# THE CHRISTMAS SONNETS

poems by

## Harald Wyndham

prints by

## Linda Wolfe

# THE CHRISTMAS SONNETS

poems by Harald Wyndham
prints by Linda Wolfe

ISBN number: 0-937179-11-6

Copyright, 1996, Blue Scarab Press

All rights to the prints aside from their appearance in this book are returned and belong to Linda Wolfe.

Sonnets I through X were published in CHEAP MYSTERIES, by Harald Wyndham, copyright 1981. They have been edited and revised for this edition.

Sonnets XI through XXIII were published in HEAVENLY RHYTHM AND BLUES, by Harald Wyndham, Copyright 1993 by Blue Scarab Press. They have been edited and revised for this edition.

Sonnets 24 and 25 have not been previously published in a collection.

Sonnets 23 and 24 were written as Christmas carols. The music was composed by the author and is printed on pages 55 through 57.

THE CHRISTMAS SONNETS was manufactured by Litho Printing and published by Blue Scarab Press on November 1, 1996.

Please address all correspondence to BLUE SCARAB PRESS
243 S. 8th Avenue, Pocatello, Idaho 83201

To the Spirit of Christmas

and all in whom it lives


To the Child in the manger

and all who gather round

*Venite adoramus, Christi*

*Kyrie eliason*

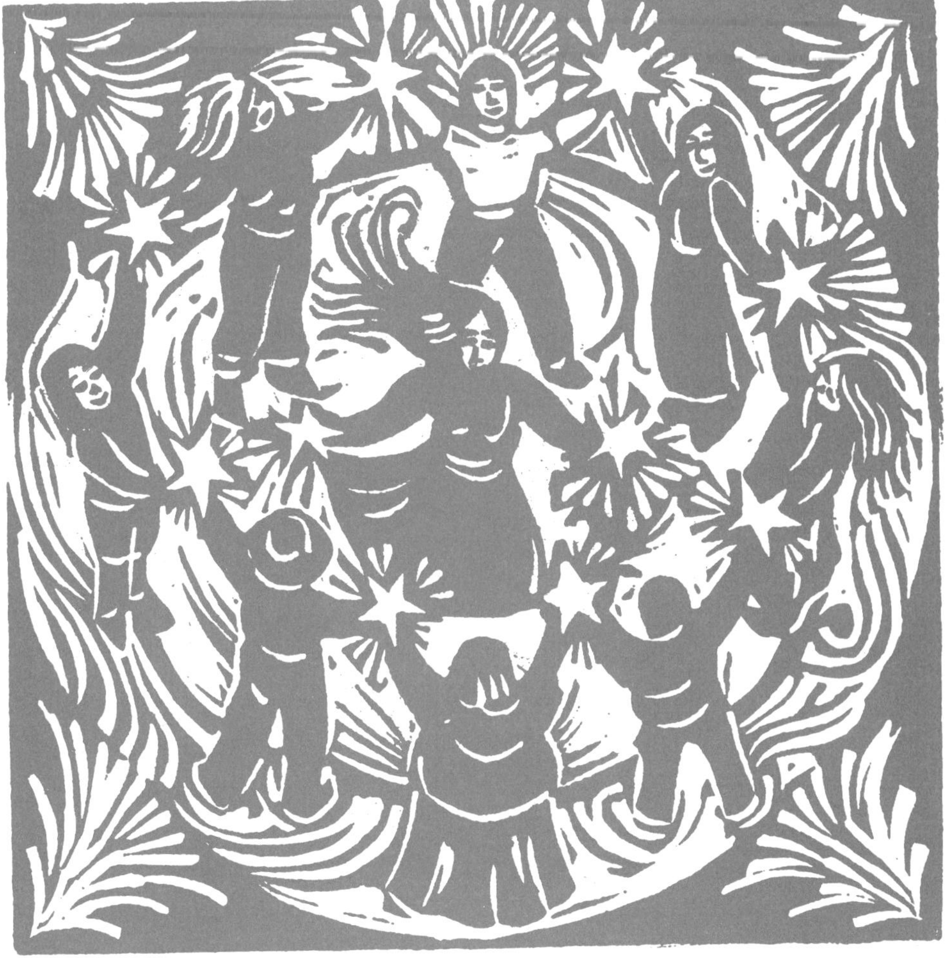

# I

Now let the year come to a glorious end!
With singing and glad faces let us dance!
Deck the dark green tree with colored lights
and decorate our hearts with memories!
Let the Child in everyone be born--
fill bowls with sweetmeats, figs and dates--
set candy and fruitcake out for all to share,
and let each window glow with candlelight!
Labor late at night on handmade gifts.
Hide secrets in each special hidden place.
Polish the family silver, burnish the brass--
sing carols together round the old upright--
then go to church, no matter what your faith.
Be filled with God's Good News this Holy Night!

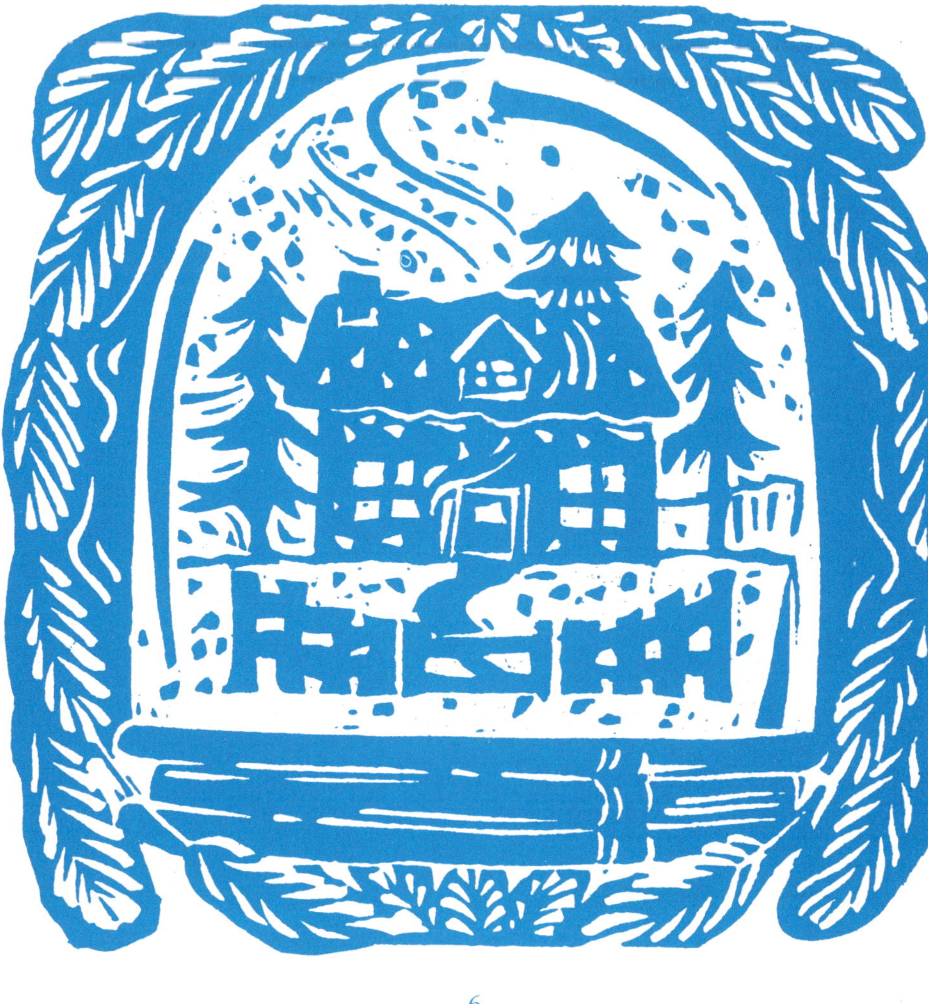

## II

Now in the dying year's darkest hour,
the heart makes room for those who are not here,
and lights a candle for each missing face,
sending, instead of gifts, a prayer:

*May He who has designed us all embrace*
*our solitary journeys with His Grace.*
*May wings of comfort mercifully guide*
*each weary traveler to his resting place.*
*May we, in dazzled silence, stand beside*
*the cradle of the Christchild, who died*
*on the body's bitter crucifix to raise*
*Love's holy tree in every heart this Christmastide.*

Come--with glad voices--each heart ablaze--
let us sing! Celebrate! Dance him for twelve days!

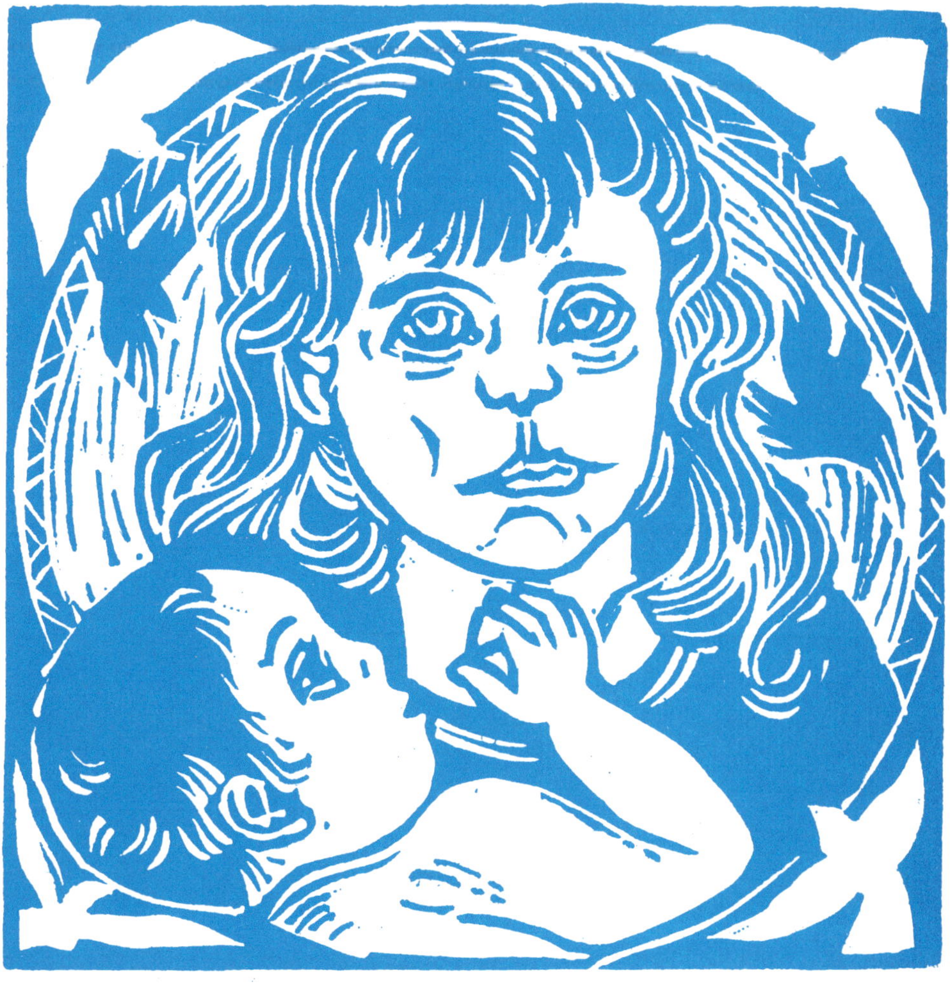

## III

"Good Christian Men Rejoice!" the carol says.
"Welcome the Newborn King--the Ancient of Days!"
Once born, He is reborn again each year,
slaughtered again each year that we might be
renewed in hope, released from mortal fear
and dance in ritual round the double tree.

The Tree of Life we light this night with joy
becomes, in three months time, the instrument
of painful sacrifice for Mary's infant boy
(in whose name we all our sins repent).
Sing canticle and Christmas lullaby
with gladsome voices, brimming with good cheer!
*Christus!* Enter us tonight!   Noel!  Noel!

All this from our outpost at the edge of hell.

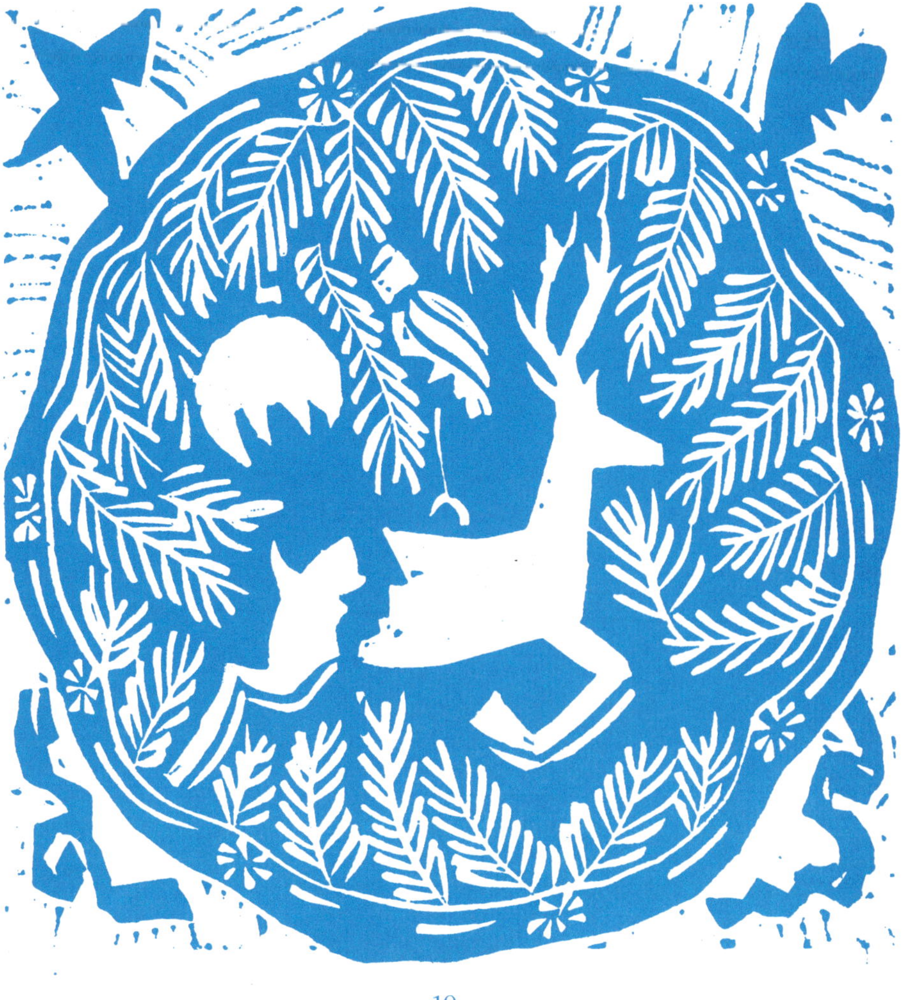

## IV

Sweet Jesus, I am tired of Christmas.

I am tired of wrapping presents,
tired of making little surprises.
Thank God there are no relatives to visit.
Thank God for peace and quiet for a few hours.

Christmas must be firstborn in the heart.
I need an afternoon or two of solitude.
I need to walk among the frosted tombstones,
down silent corridors of frozen trees.
I need the crunch of snow beneath my boots,
the healing pleasure of wielding a stick.

*Christus! Christus!* My heart has no place for Thee.

It is as empty as a gravel lane
with only a few broken branches lying there.

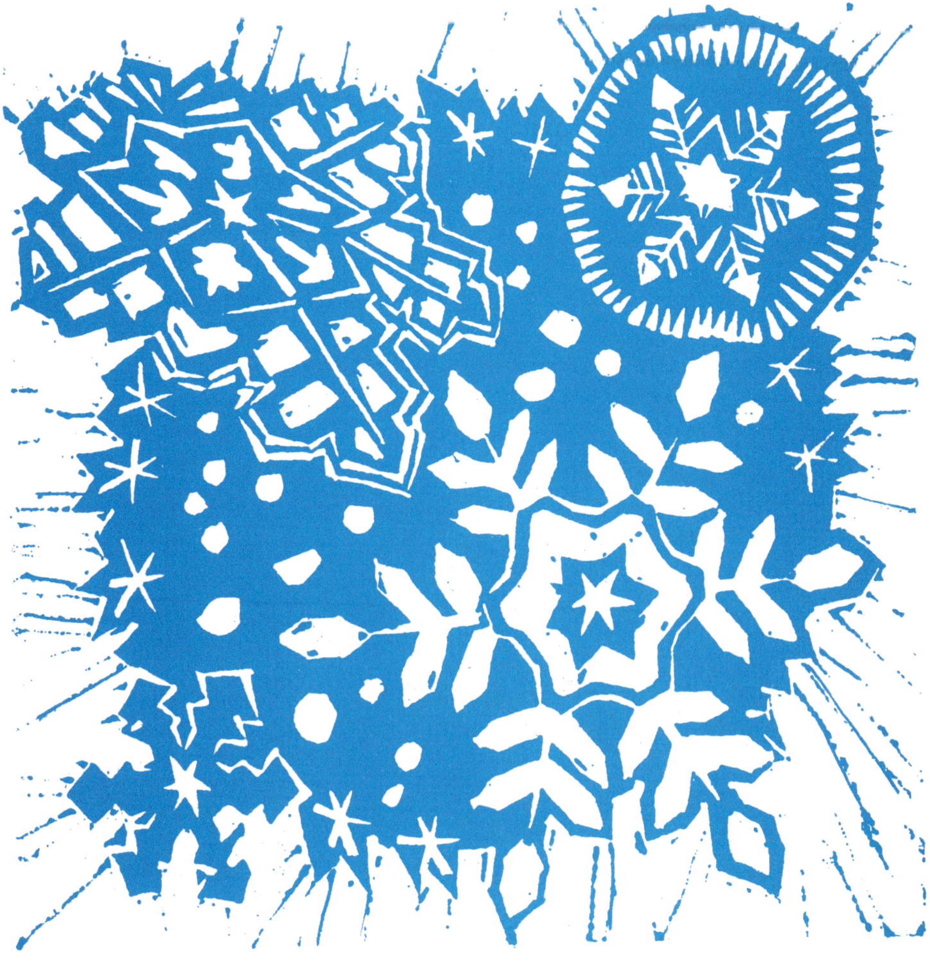

## V

God's purest mystery
comes like fresh snow in the night,
blanketing the heart worn tired with compromising,
filling the mind with drifts of memory,
transforming the world.

That we might rise and go forth in the daylight--
New People!  Reborn in spirit!
Singing anthems to the perfect Lord
whose gift falls freely
on the rooftops of all people,
to make morning beautiful,
to cover us with Peace beyond understanding,

that we might love each other
for a little while . . .

14

## VI

The deep snow hides the house, the night is still.
The children put their shoes in the windowsill.
It is St. Nicholas Eve.  The saint will dole
to every child some candy or some coal.

Soft carols mull the air, the fire dies.
Time gathers to a teardrop in my eye.
Melt a frosty circle on the glass.
Tonight a Christmas mystery will pass.

The streets are desolate, the sky is dark.
The stars stand out like phosphorescent sparks.
My children snuggle down in their small beds.
Christmas comes for children, it is said.

*Dear Christchild--come to me now if you will.*
*I leave my empty soul on the windowsill.*

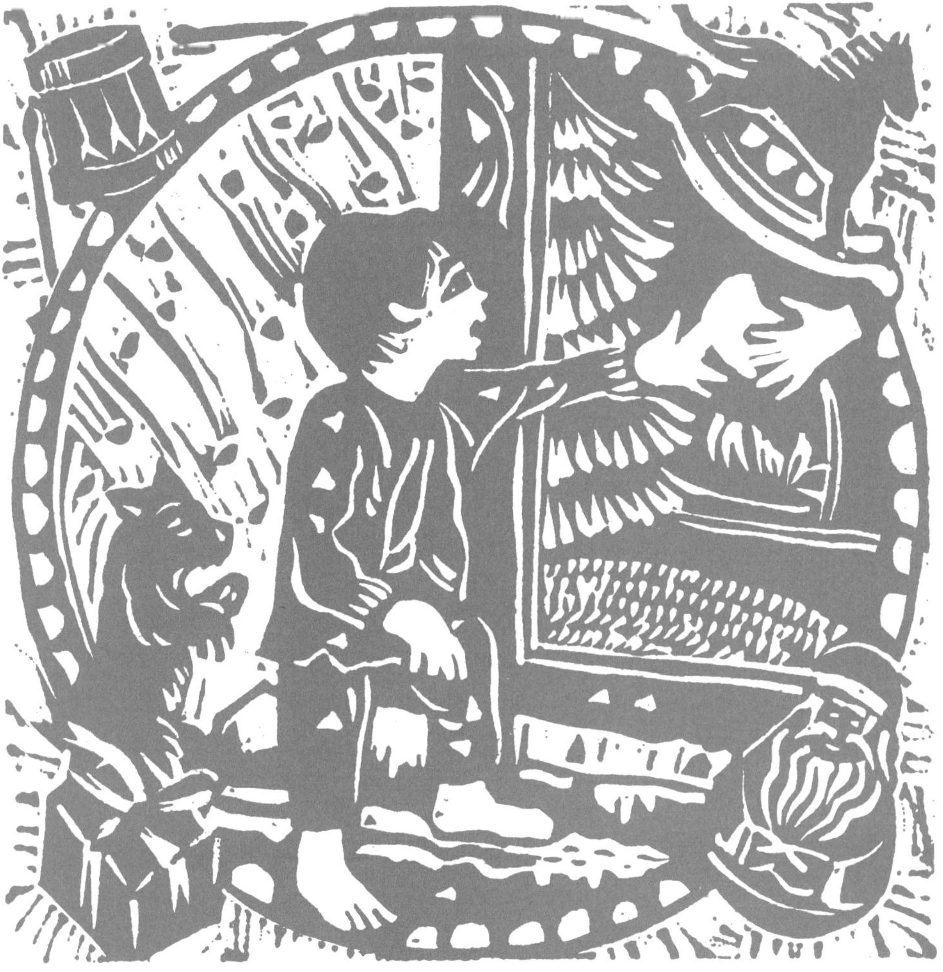

## VII

For all who are lonesome and far from home,
who press against cold windows in the night,
*pray for us Mother, now and at the hour of our birth.*

For the smug, indifferent ones, who have it made
and cannot hear disaster rushing the door,
*pray for us, dear Mother, at the hour of our birth.*

For children, whose clear eyes and vulnerable souls
are offered up each day on the butcher's block,
*have mercy, Mother, now and at the hour of our birth.*

For every soul that founders in the void
and falls down helpless, reaching for a hand,
*dear Mother of God at the hour of our birth we pray--*

Be near to us, be near to those we love--
as if we each were Jesus, born this day.

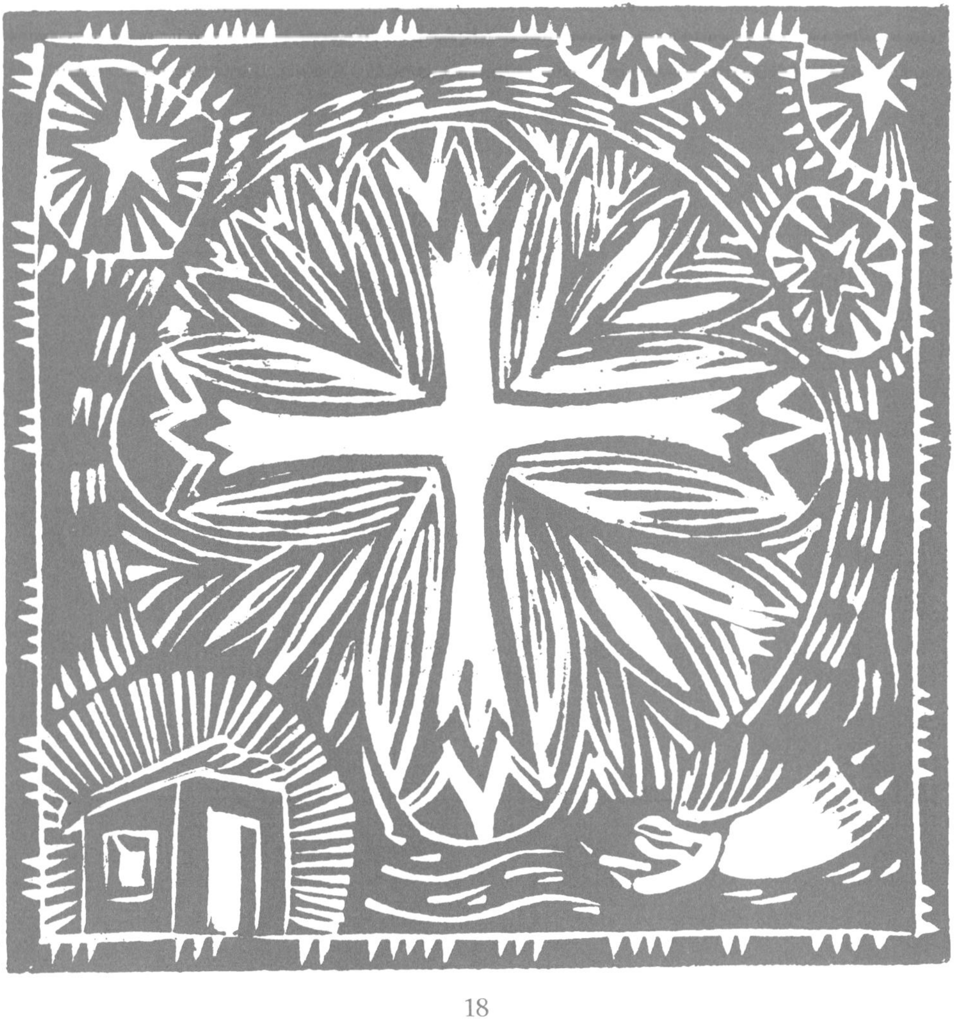

## VIII

Of all the stars we dream of, there is one
so rare and beautiful the noonday sun
cannot compare in brilliance, yet its light
escapes the finest telescopic sight
(which proves the argument of pessimists--
that such a dream-like star does not exist).

And truly, as I walk the crowded street,
the cold, flourescent universe stripped bare
of every human feeling, save despair,
I find no star in any face I meet,
just sullen weariness and nervous care--
the masses struggling homeward in defeat.

*O! Now is the time for Christmas, let it start!*
*The Star of Bethlehem bursting every heart!*

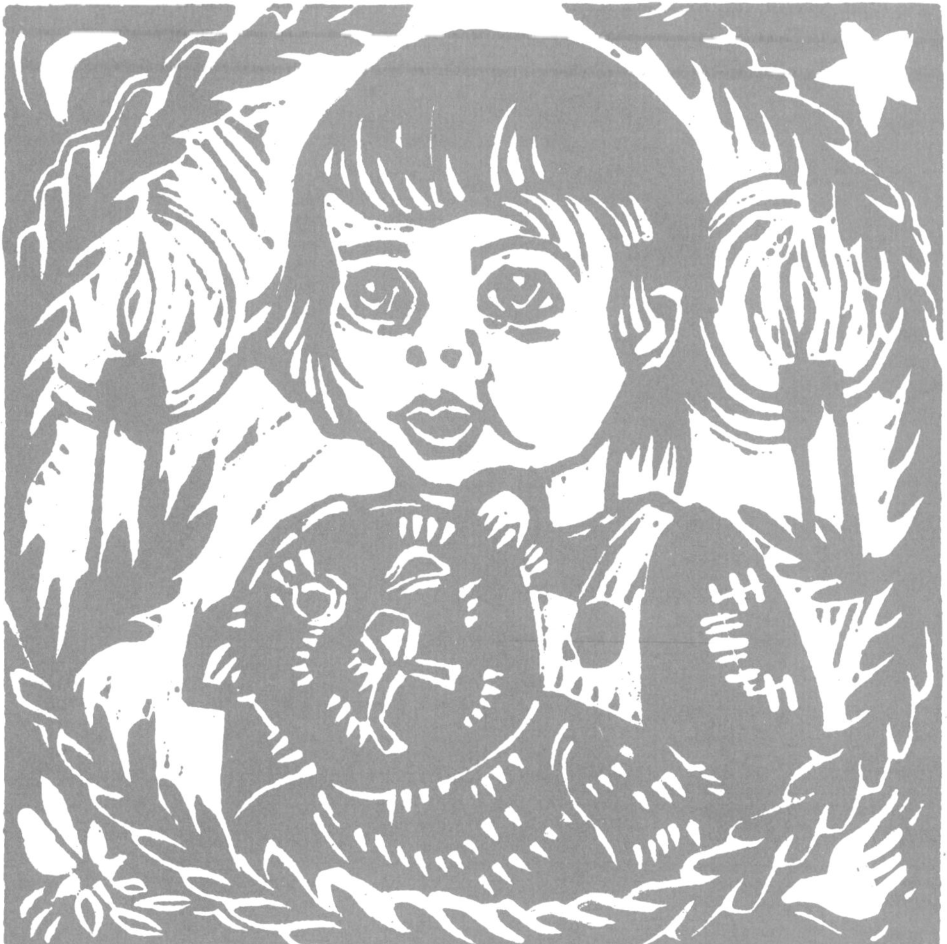

## IX

Tiny Jesu -- Holy Child of light!
Be born in every heart this Christmas night!
Descend like snowfall blanketing our sins
with your redeeming mercy, soft and white.

The creature we created crouches within,
lonely for the love of another person.
With angry tears it cries itself to sleep.
Transform this creature into child again!

Dear little savior--come like snowfall deep
to fill us with excitement--a joyous leap
outside ourselves toward others--
our lives unwrapped like gifts for them to keep!

*Jesus, help us love all men as brothers.*
*Jesus, keep us from destroying each other.*

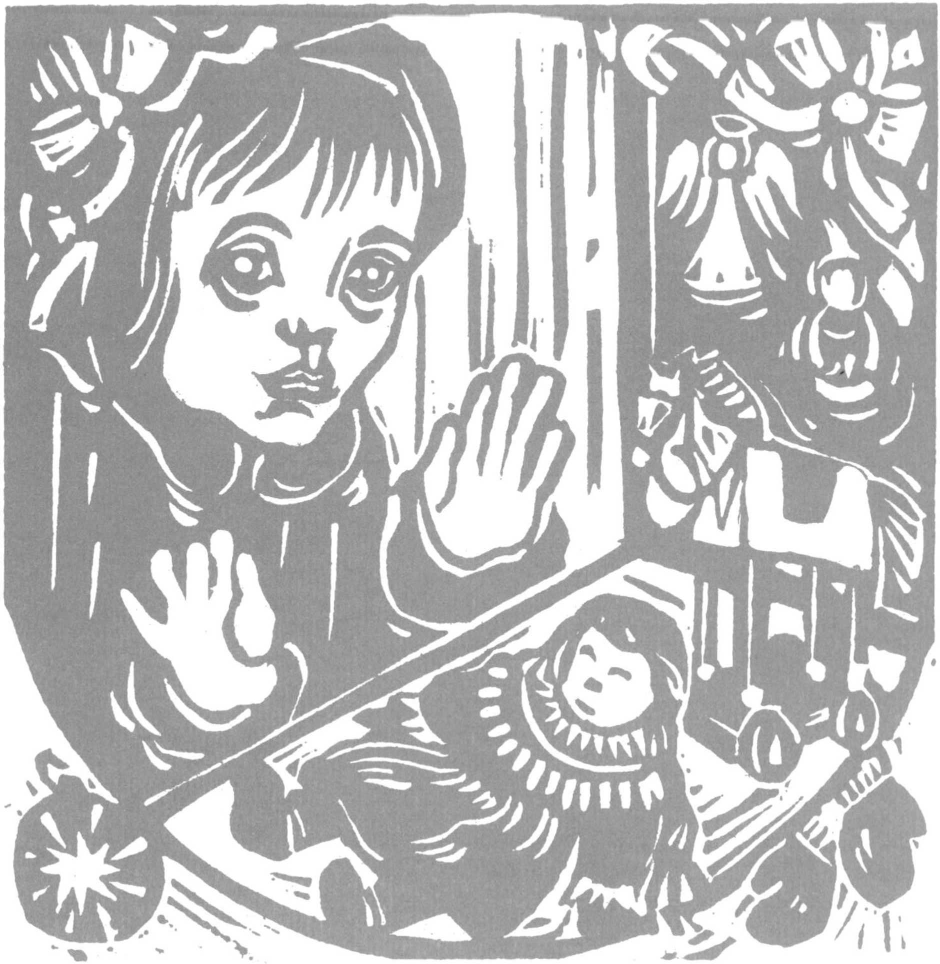

## X

Dear child of love, the year comes back to you.
Twelve months we've done the worst that we could do
to make you hate our race.

                             We have not ceased
to kill each other, rape, steal, accuse and blame
the innocent, carelessly calling you by name
to curse all those we fear.

                             There is no peace
on earth, Lord. We spit in your face, abuse
the children we are charged to keep, devise
all manner of fine rhetoric to excuse
our failures.

                 Are you not tired of our lies?
Are you not finally angered beyond all love?
What we have done no jury would forgive.

*And yet you come again, this Christmas night,*
*blessing the darkened world with perfect light.*

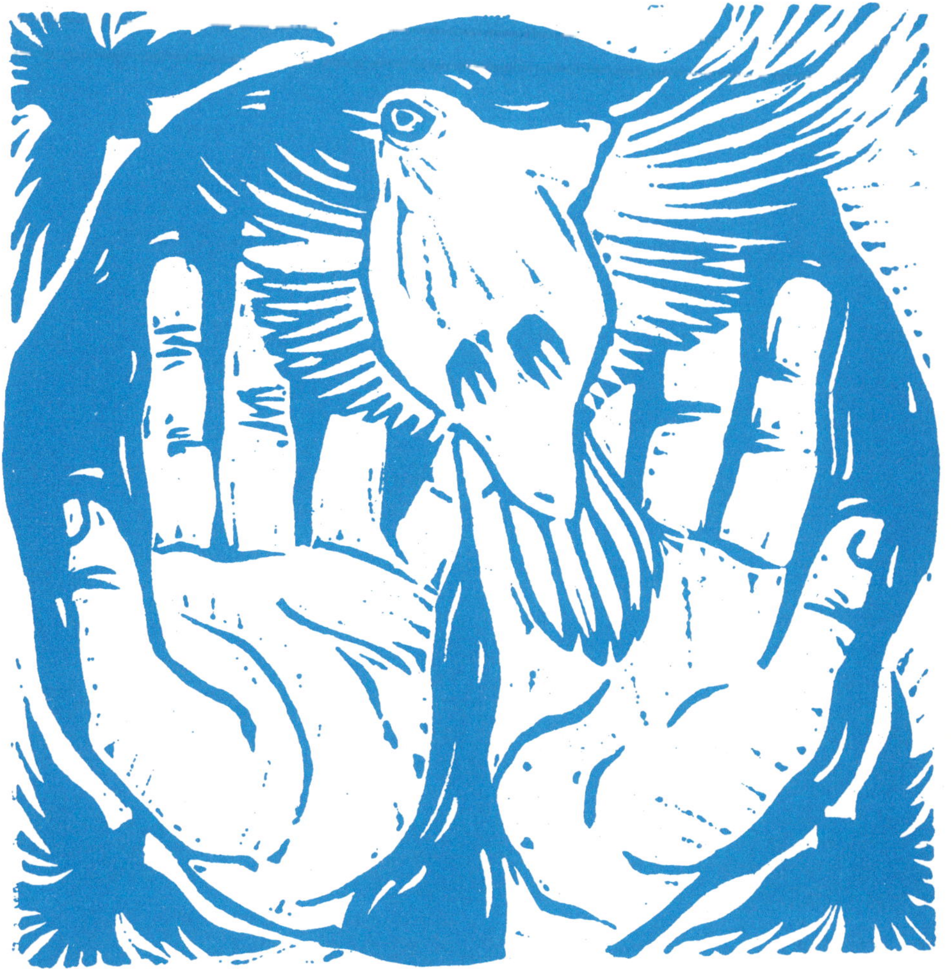

## XI

I took a Christmas walk in a bitter storm.
Bundled and scarved, I braved the smashing wind,
trudging through heavy drifts as soft as sin
and shouting out carols to keep my spirits warm.

The wind cut to the bone and I was tired
of struggling against the subtle weight of snow,
battling a gale that shattered my bravest song,
and so I rested beneath an evergreen.

Protected from the worst the wind could do,
I found the silence that my soul desired.
The tree stood solid as the hand of God,
creating stillness in the midst of storm.

*The Holy Spirit spoke its Living Word,*
*and in my heart the Christchild was born.*

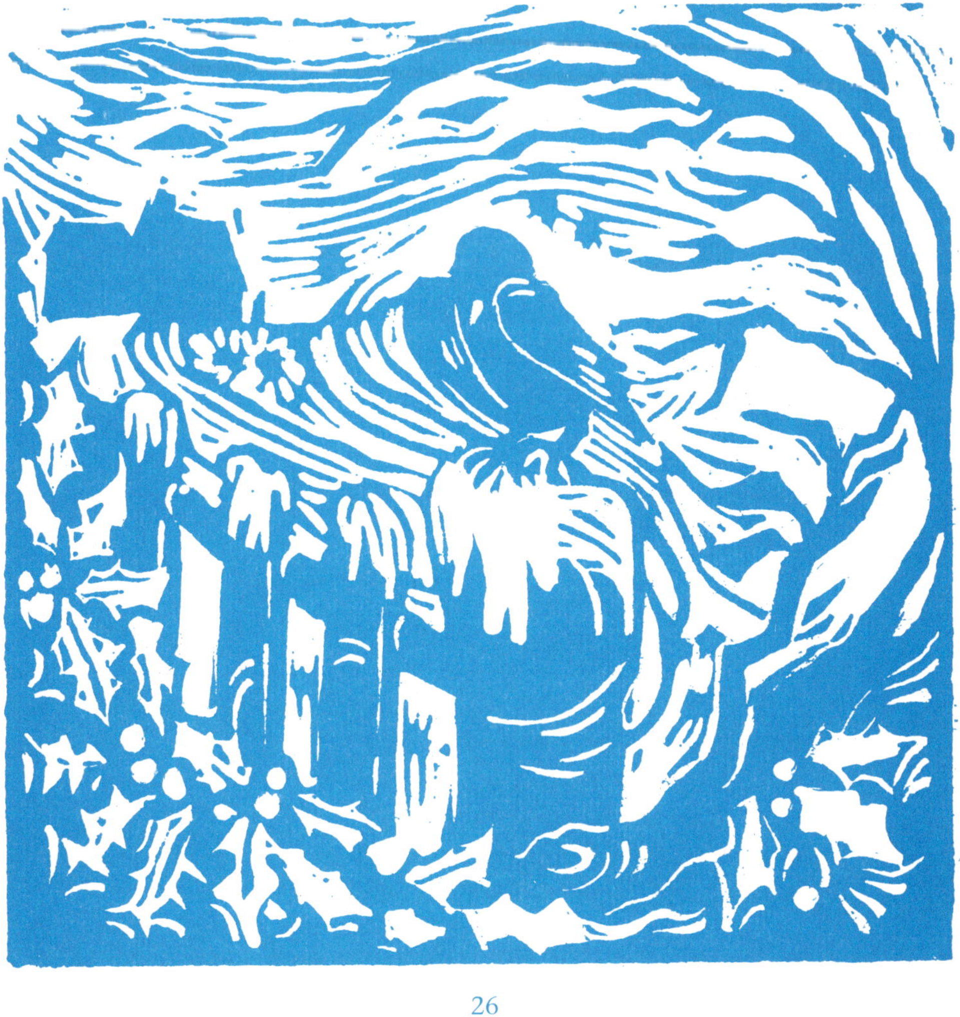

## XII

Out of our world of weapons, war and disease,
*we yearn for you, Lord Jesus, Prince of Peace.*

Out of exhaustion, weary of conflict and strife,
*we hunger for you Jesus, Bread of Life.*

Out of our fear of sacrifice, out of our greed,
*we remember you, Lord Jesus, Lamb of God.*

Out of the sickness that wastes us without and within,
*we pray to you, Lord Jesus, Healer of Men.*

Out of our ignorance, out of deep moral distress,
*we turn to you, Jesus, Teacher of Righteousness.*

Out of despair with our lives--empty, absurd--
*we ache for you, Lord Jesus, Living Word.*

In expectation with people all over the earth,
*we gather round you, Jesus, at your birth.*

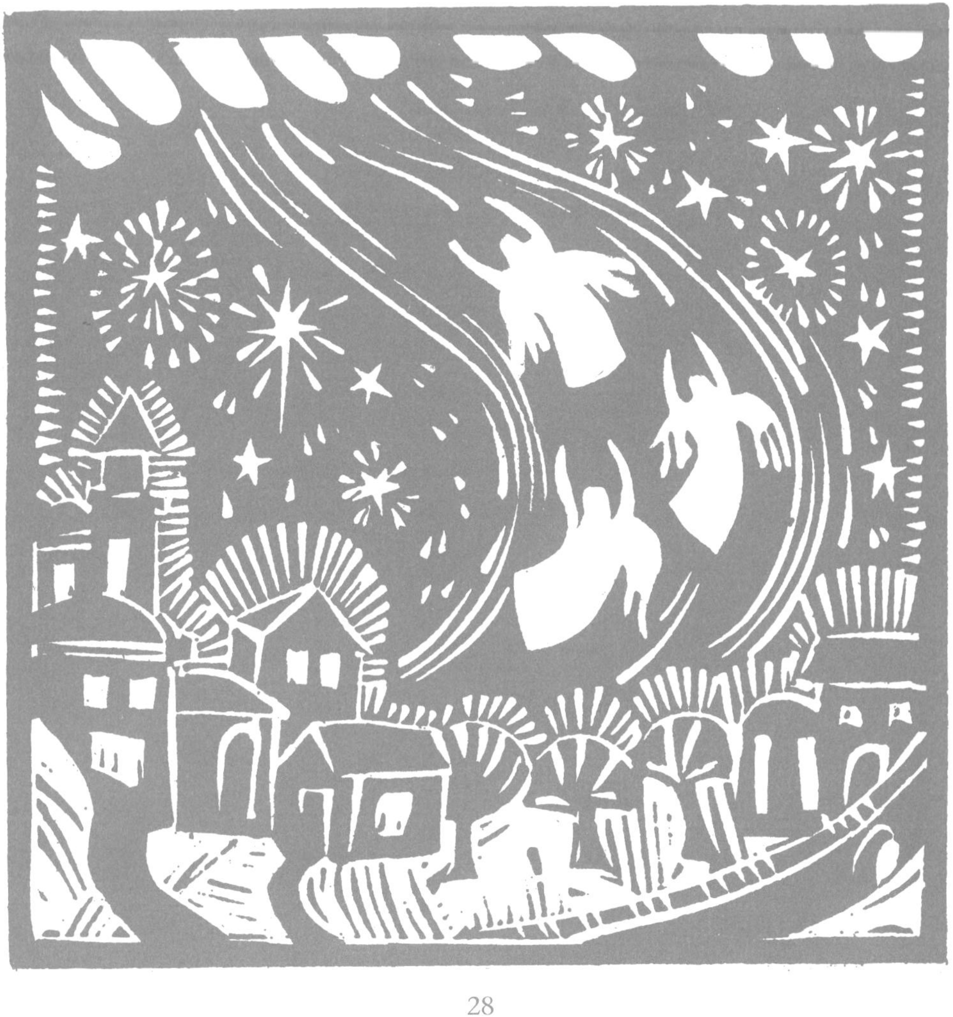

## XIII

Oh dark, dark, dark, dark and dark
is this poor, broken world tonight.
The threat of holocaust holds us by the throat,
and terror roams our streets with random bombs.
The prisoners of power enslave the poor,
and money and illusion rule the rest.

*Now--from the Living God--a Living Word!*
*Love! Love! Love! Love and Love!*

Jesus Christ is born! He is alive!
He lives in all who turn to Him in need.
Beyond all doctrines and beyond dispute,
beyond the prison bars of mind and heart,
His all-forgiving love, made flesh tonight,

*is Light--pure Light--unquenchable, living Light!*

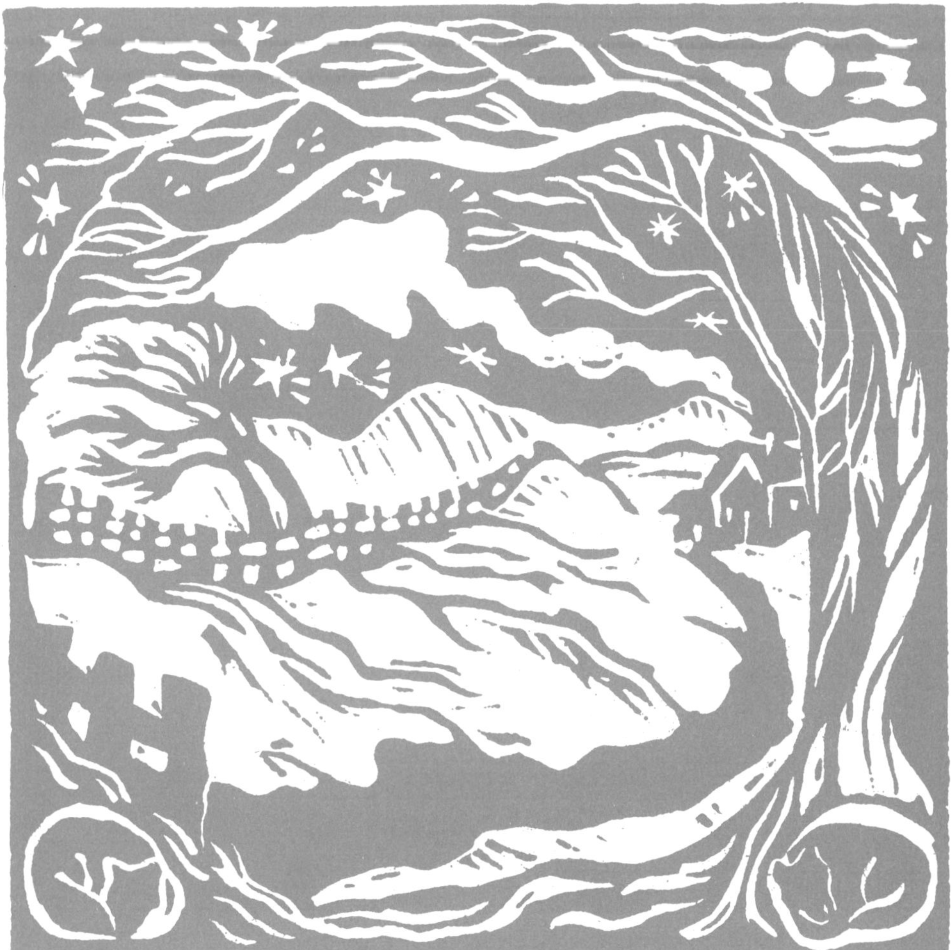

## XIV

O cover the earth, Lord--cover it like snow.
Come in the darkness when we are asleep.
Transform the world with whiteness soft and deep.
Transform us also, as we dream and grow.

When we awake, Lord, let us be new persons--
no longer angry or bitter, overwhelmed with pride.
Overwhelm us with your love instead,
that we might live each day in your kingdom.

Tonight especially, this Christmas night,
O vast, mysterious Father, Creator and Lord,
be present here among us--speak Thy Word--
gather us speechless before Thy Perfect Light.

*The light of Jesus, in whom we are reborn,*
*be both our daily bread and daily passion.*

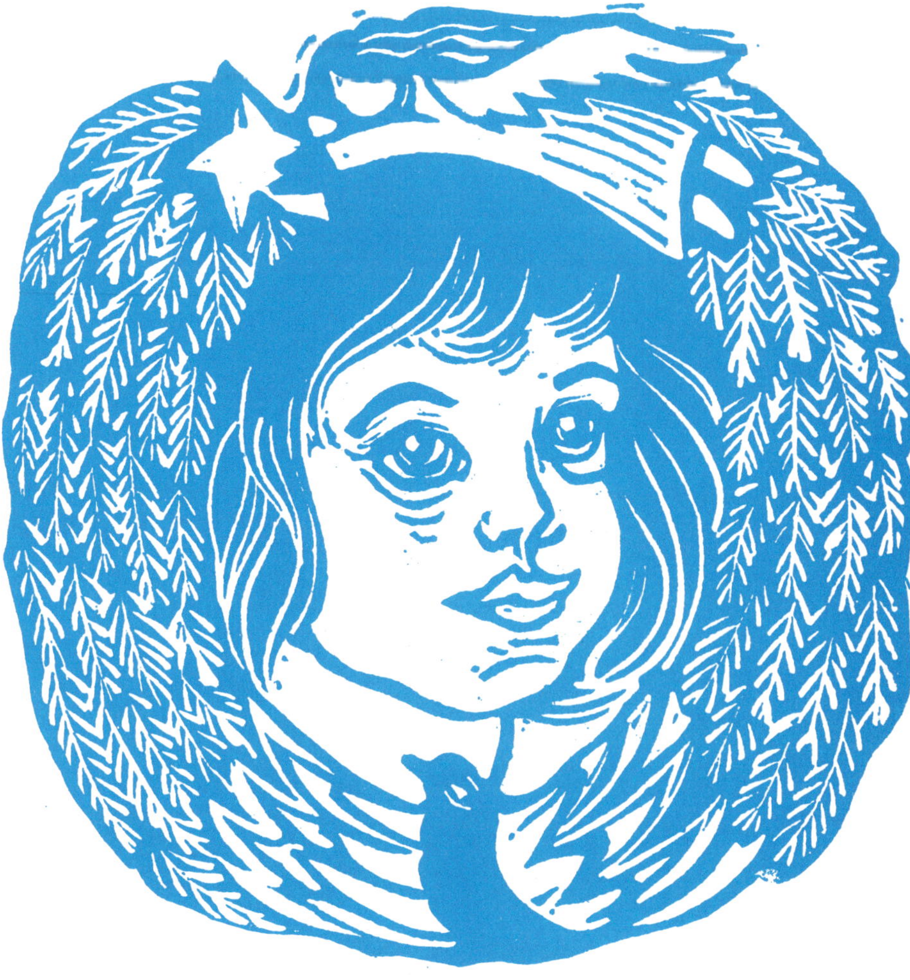

## XV

Each evening I walk out in the snow
to tour the neighborhood transformed with lights,
the houses twinkling with an inner glow
of cheerful celebration--wreath on the door,
festive tree in the livingroom window--
and I am pleased (against the dark of night)
to notice that the homes of rich and poor
are equally made beautiful and bright.

So it is when Jesus enters the heart
to stand within us like a glowing tree.
His perfect light casts out all fear of dark
and spreads into the night for all to see,
that strangers pushing toward some distant place
might find the Christchild in a human face.

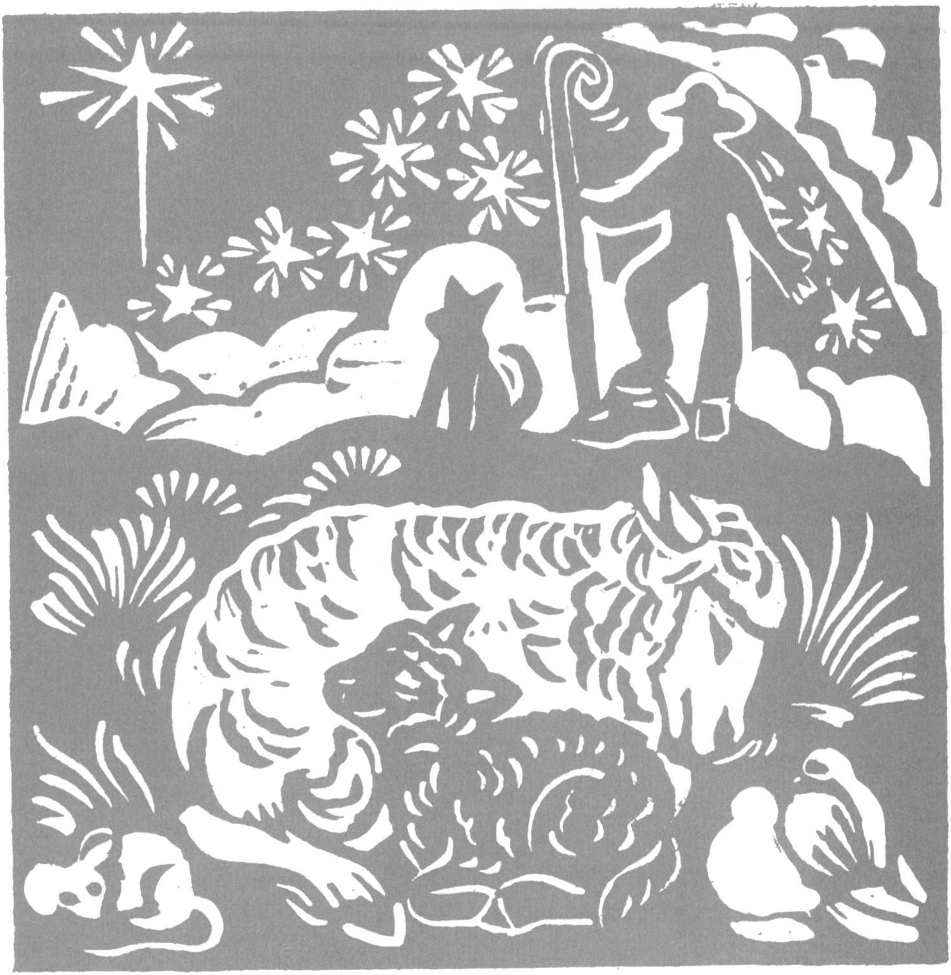

## XVI

When God entered into His creation,
risking the vulnerability of the flesh,
He did not come as King of all the nations,
the Prince of Power, conceived among the rich,
but rather as the poorest of the poor.
To common folk who struggle for a living,
He came to know the hardship, share the chores,
and experience for himself the pain of loving.

To Mary then--a simple, honest girl--
to Bethlehem and to Nazareth was born
the King of Kings, rejected by the world,
the Lord of Lords, who wears a crown of thorns,
the Prince of Peace, the Shepherd of the lost,
who carries all creation on a cross.

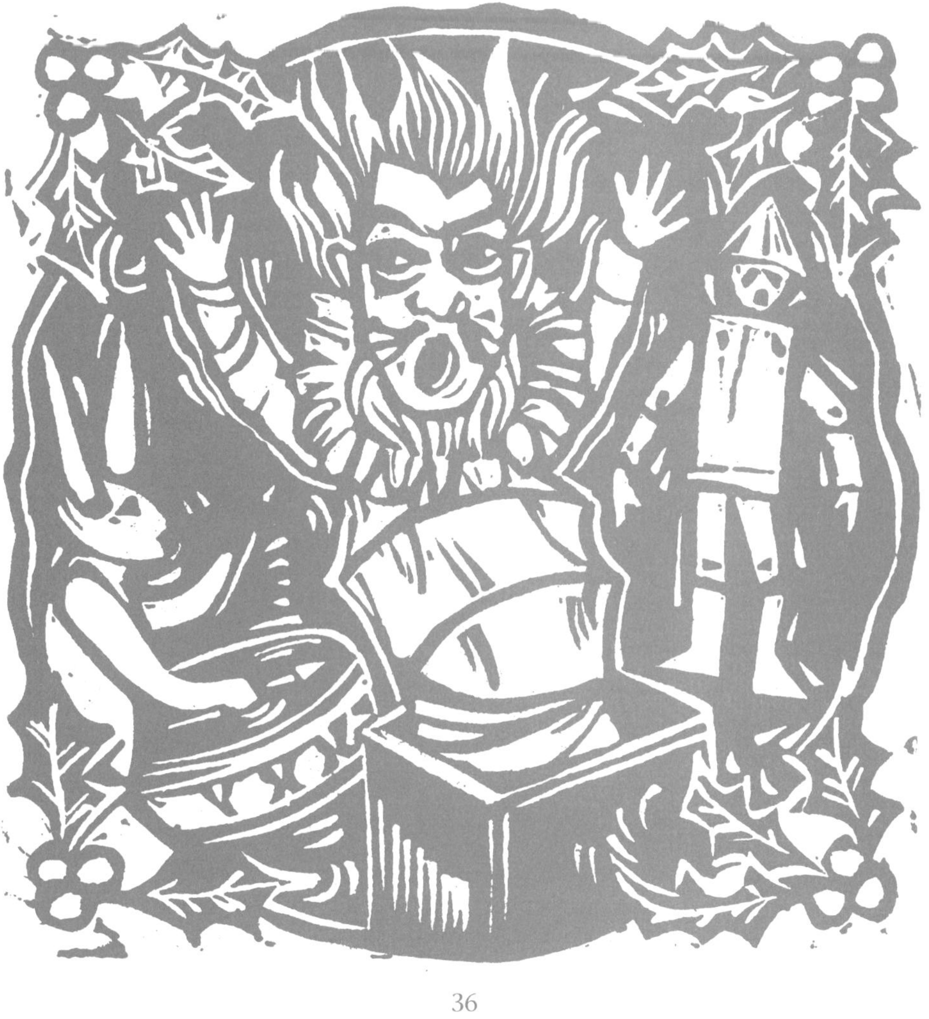

## XVII

To see His birth in the birth of every creature
is to be religious.  Not to see Him at all
is to be profane.  We live and die
by how we see the world--bless and kill
by what we choose to know--God's Truth
made flesh for us in human faces.

Though princes of the world preach might is right
and smooth-tongued preachers sell a cheap salvation,
the hard wind scatters them all like leaves.
Nature, unornamented as a tree, receives
our tiny gods like Christmas decorations.
The Lord arrives like fresh snow in the night.

*Each living being contains all mysteries.*
*Approach each other, therefore, on your knees.*

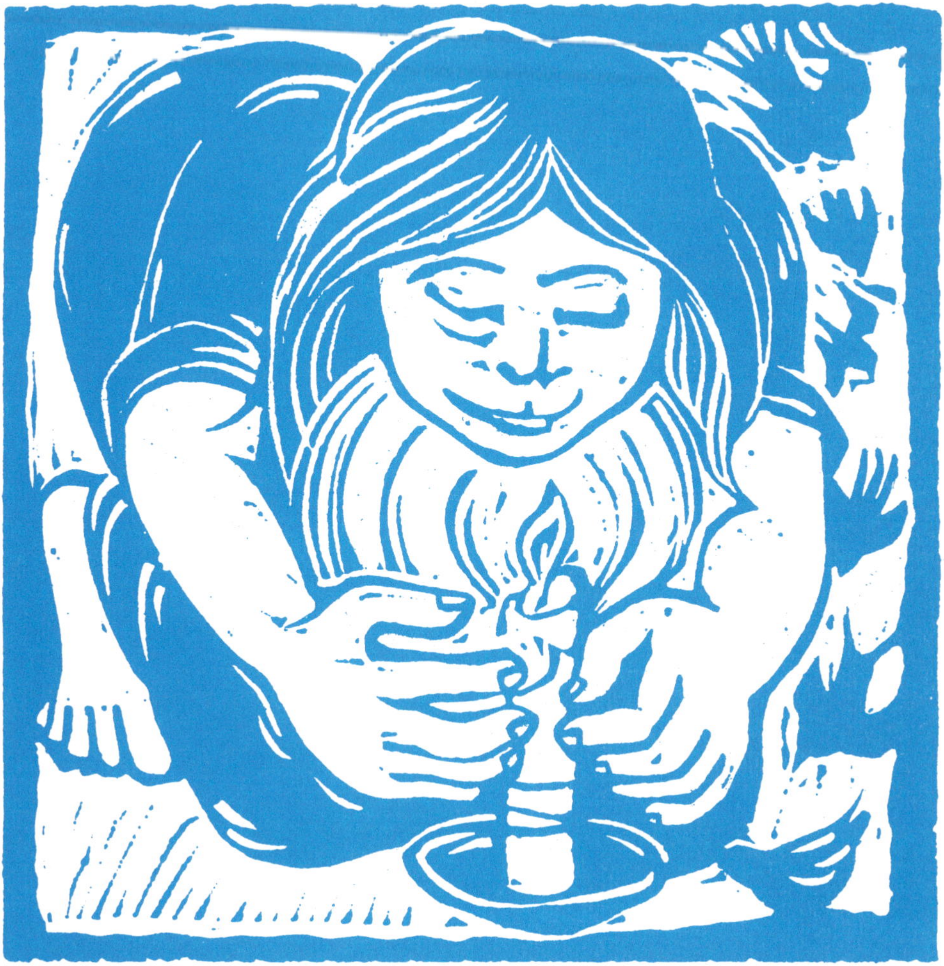

## XVIII

All children come from God.  The power
to create human life is His, not ours.

Ours is to receive the precious gift
(flesh of our flesh, naked and helpless)
to care for with all joy and tenderness,
with discipline that is love's handicraft,
modeling mercy and demonstrating truth
despite our shortcomings.
                                To be completely there--
feeding, teaching, sheltering from harm,
suffering the unfair arrogance of youth
with godgiven patience that all parents share,
(the old man wrapping the prodigal in his arms)
this is the highest calling in the world--

*to see in every child the Christchild.*

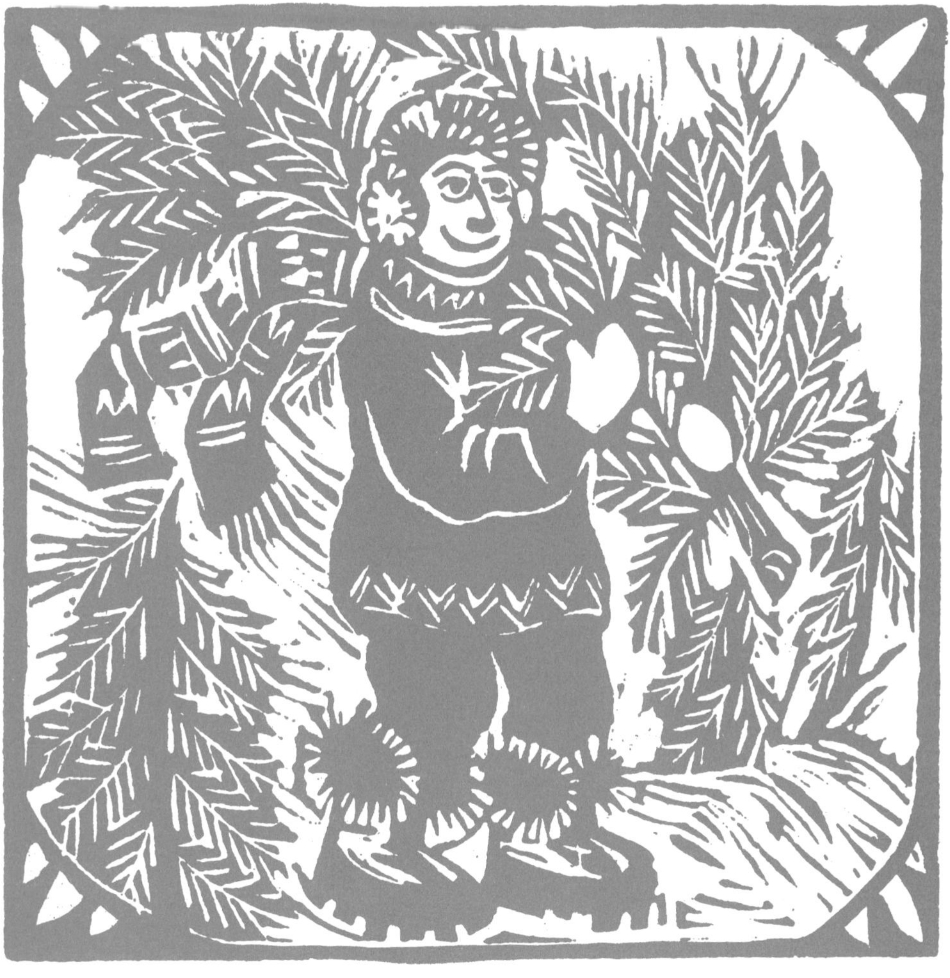

## XIX

*We cradle round the tree of memories.*

Long years after childhood is gone,
our parents gone, the children grown and gone,
the long walk after dark through snowbound streets,
beneath bright stars that reaffirm our dreams--
the box of handmade, fragile ornaments,
the colored lights and wooden crucifix,
two painted angels and a manger scene.

This glowing center of the midnight room--
a candled, caroled, memory-laden tree--
is rooted in a longing old as time:
to be alive forever in the mind,
to be with those we love, and safe from harm.

*To be the Christchild, rocked in Mary's arms.*

42

## XX

In the barren winter, snowswept and bleak,
the heart opens its storehouse of good gifts
and entertains the Christchild in each guest,
spreading the snow with sunflowers for the birds,
with nuts and apples for the hungry squirrels.

We think about the hungry of the world,
about the millions that we cannot feed,
and how there is no war in wintertime
when frost reminds us of our fragile lives
and how, but for earth's greenness, we would die.

In winter solitude we dream of peace,
a place to sleep in front of a warm fire,
where we forgive the injuries of the year
and are thankful just to be alive.

## XXI

Walking with the dog one winter night,
worn out by overwork and by the world,
I heard a raucous, unexpected cry
and saw a flock of snowgeese in the sky.

Their ranks were ragged, not an arrowhead,
but more a half-bent bow of beating wings,
struggling west against the coming storm
and calling to each other for encouragement.

I felt their weariness and caught their hope--
the snowswept grainfields finally in sight.
I thought of winged, angelic messengers
proclaiming wondrous news one starry night.

*I thought about the long-awaited child.*

Then turned to face the bitter wind--and smiled.

46

## XXII

The Child among us--the long-awaited Child!
Child with eyes of innocence open wide
who looks into our faces without fear,
without prejudice or hatred, accepting each one,
whatever our age, our history, our color--whatever we are--
this Child looks into our faces and sees what we are,
swims deep in the pool of our hearts and touches us,
this Child of God, dreamed of for so many years,
come in the night in this unexpected place,
this place of poverty transformed into joy
by the eyes of this Child accepting all that we are,
our pitiful mistakes invisible, our sins unseen,
the world transformed and reborn and surrounded
     with peace
in the eyes of this long dreamed of Child of God
     with us at last!

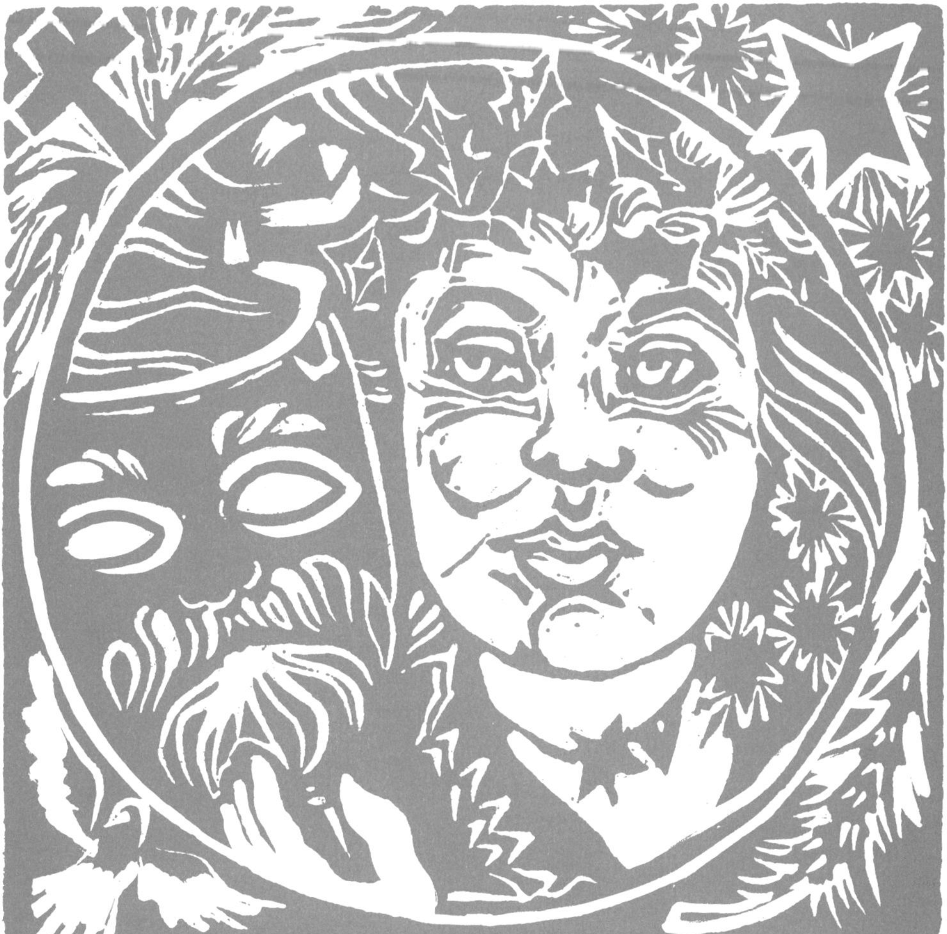

## XXIII *

A.

God was not born in a church or cathedral,
God was not born in a temple or a mosque.
Rather God came as a blessing to all people,
born in a manger in a stable in the rocks.

God did not come to the king and the rulers,
God did not come to the wealthy and the strong.
Rather God came to the wise men and shepherds,
and to the people who'd been waiting for so long.

B.

God did not come to the white people only,
rather to all men and women, yellow, red and brown.
God came to comfort the poor and the lonely,
and to free the prisoner unjustly put down.

C.

God became a baby, helpless and wonderful.
Yeshua Immanuel, born in Bethlehem.

* To be sung in the style of a Hebrew folksong
  *Music on page 55*

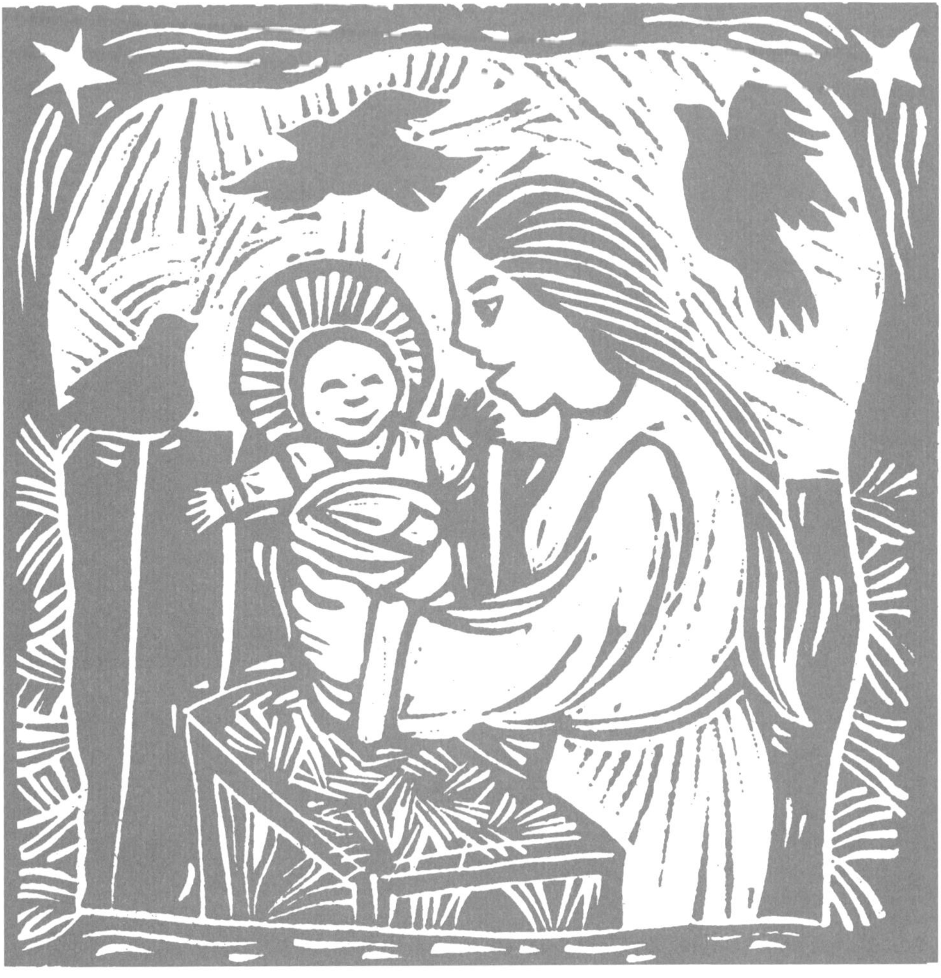

## XXIV *

Look at the Christchild, lying in the manger,
Look at the Mother, loving and tender,

Look at the shepherds, fresh from the night,
Listen to angels, singing in starlight,

Look at the wisemen, kings of the world,
Look at them bringing gifts to the Christchild.

*Look at us Jesus, surrounding you here--*
*Look at our hunger, our hopes and our tears . . .*

Look at the Savior washed in the Jordan,
Look at Him tempted, wrestling with Satan,

Look at Him feeding bodies and minds,
Look at Him healing the lame and the blind,

Look at the Mother, broken with loss,
Look at the Savior, hung on the cross . . . Ah!

*\* To be sung as a carol--music on pages 56-57*

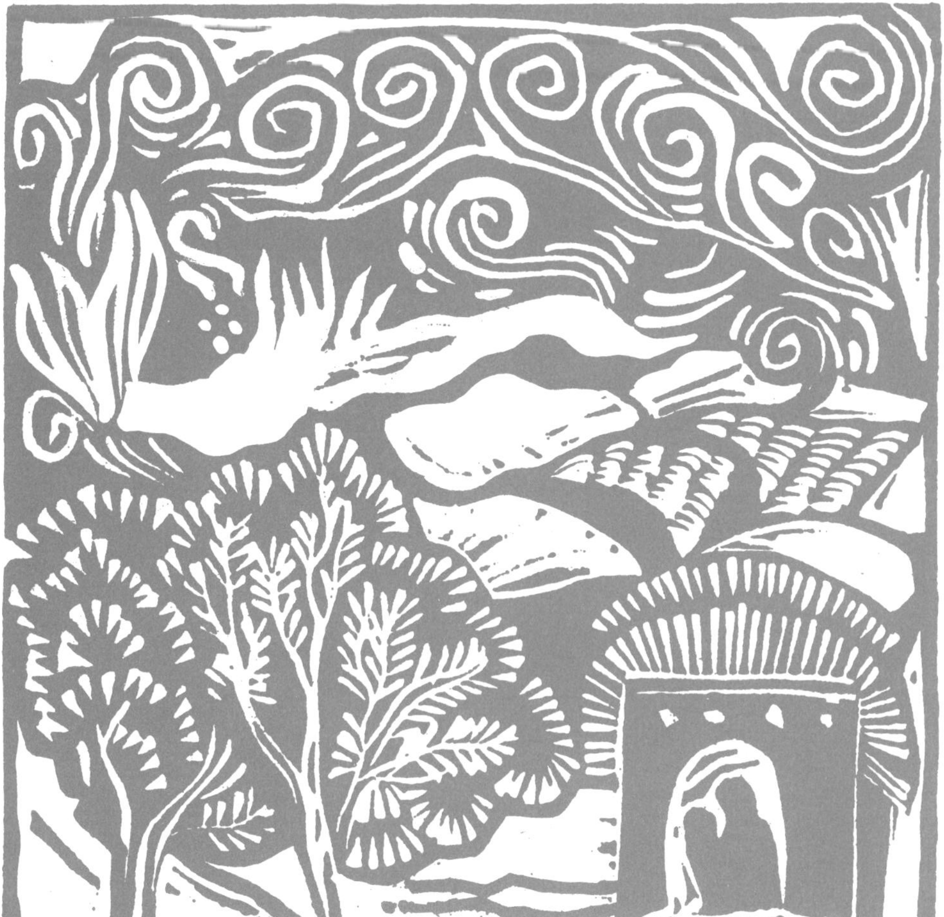

## XXV

On a cold, winter night the Christchild comes,
In a small, quiet place, hidden from men.
While outside the world is on fire with fear,
with earthquakes, diseases, disaster and war,
inside the stable the stillness is warm.
To Mary and Joseph, the Christchild comes.

To shepherds and angels the Christchild comes,
surrounded by creatures and wonder and songs.
While outside a whirlwind of woe fills the skies,
with robbery and murder, betrayal and lies,
inside the stable, in Mary's warm arms,
to poor, sinful people the Christchild comes.

*The Christchild comes on a dark winter night,*
*bringing healing, forgiveness and mercy and light.*

# XXIII

# XXIV

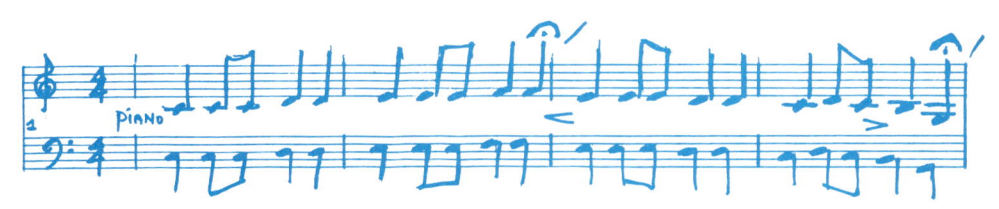

Look at the Christchild, lying in the manger, Look at the Mother, loving and tender,

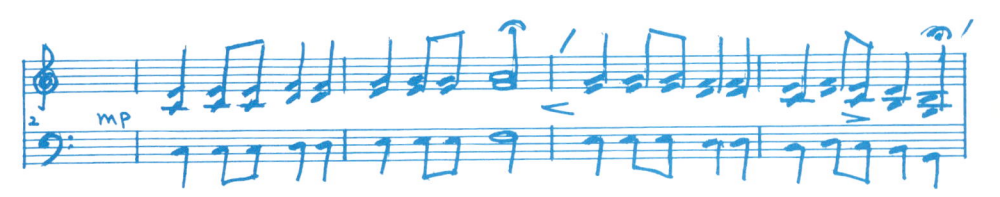

Look at the shepherds, fresh from the night, Listen to angels, singing in starlight,

Look at the wise men, kings of the world, Look at them bringing gifts to the Christchild,

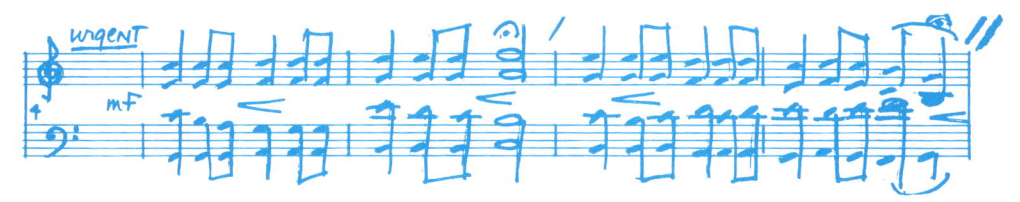

Look at us Jesus, surrounding you here, Look at our hunger, our hopes and our tears . . .

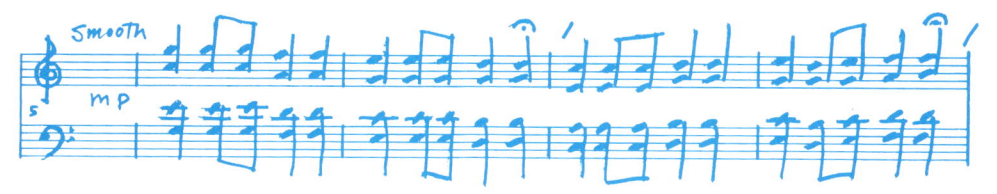

Look at the Savior washed in the Jordan, Look at Him tempted, wrestling with Satan,

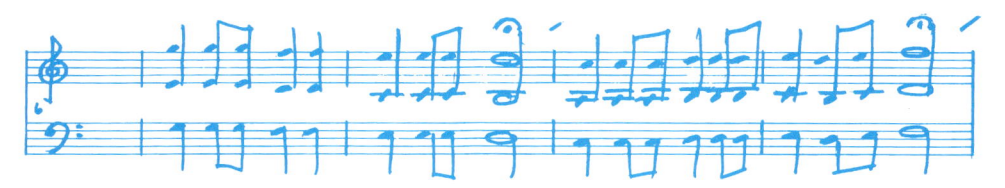

Look at Him feeding bodies and minds, Look at Him healing the lame and the blind,

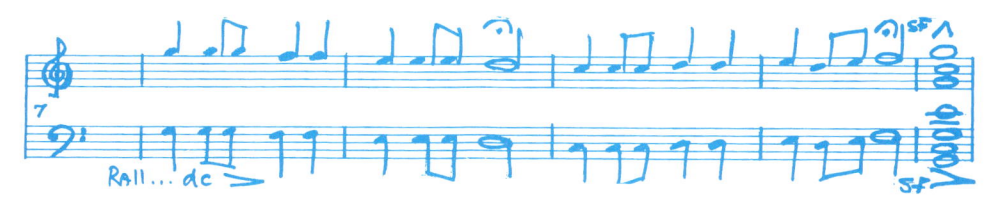

Look at the Mother, broken with loss, Look at the Savior, hung on the cross.   Ah!

## ABOUT THE POEMS

THE CHRISTMAS SONNETS by Harald Wyndham were composed as Christmas cards beginning in 1971 when he moved with his family from Ohio to Idaho and continuing through 1995--a period of twenty five years.

The sonnets vary in style and theme, often reflecting the tenor of the year or the events of family life. Sonnets 21, 22, 23 and 24 in particular reflect on the birth of the author's first grandson, Dylan John Nollner, in 1992. The focus of most of the poems is the Christchild as symbol of the precious newness and miracle of life and our need to honor the holiness of life in all things. The season of winter is a time that reminds us of our human poverty and the closeness of death. We remember that only by the grace of returning sunlight and springtime do we live.

Poems 23 and 24 are meant to be sung. Poem 23 is a folksong in the style of a Hebrew dance, while poem 24 is a written for choral singing.

## ABOUT THE PRINTS

Linda Wolfe is a visual artist and printmaker who has collaborated with Harald Wyndham on two previous books -- THE EXILE'S PILGRIMAGE AT CHRISTMASTIDE, 1979 -- and THE FOUR SEASONS IN POCATELLO, 1995. The prints were created between June and September, 1996, on linoleum block and printed originally on mulberry paper.

The book represents a co-operative effort between two artists -- the poet and the printmaker. Each is responding to the Christmas season in a personal way. For this reason, the prints are not intended to imitate the poems, but rather stand as independent statements which often complement the mood, tone or imagery of the poems. Thus the prints and poems represent two bodies of work on one theme.

In making the prints, Linda Wolfe draws on the old tradition of the European printmakers and wood carvers, who created both prints and statues to celebrate the Christmas Season.

All blessings of the Season
Be yours!

THE CHRISTMAS SONNETS features Stone Serif typeface and was printed on Teton Warm White paper as the aspens turned gold in the hills around Pocatello, Idaho in this year of our Lord, 1996.